Ebony wings

by Sankara "Le Prince Heritier" Olama-Yai

CONTENTS

Part 2: Eclipse

Dedication

In loving memory of
My father
Bill Anderson
My grandmother

I hope these words find you

A l'orée du temps
Loin des sentiers labyrintheux des angoisses
Du quotidien: RENAÎTRE

trouver les mots qui,
Traduisent, Une   Vie,
qui, resiste
A L'usure du Temps

— Guy Olama "The Poet"

At the edge of time
Far from the labyrinthine paths of the anxieties
Of everyday life: REBIRTH

Find words that translate, A   Life,
that withstands
the wear of time

— Guy Olama "Le Poète"

Part 1: Sol

Dying suns left behind
Shriveling wings, on the ghost of
my smiling shadow

High Flight
Abandoned

The world robbed me of you.

For Bill Anderson

I heard a cry emanate
from our bathroom
That day after
your Sk ull   cracked   open
on the hawaiian pavement
The essence of your mind, spilling
out onto sunny concrete.

The world robbed me of you.

There are two of us now,
living inside me
and i [1] can't bear for you to hear
the soullessness of his laugh
or feel the torment in my tears

---

[1] *In higher level maths, an imaginary number is a complex number denoted simply by the letter "i." throughout this book, i've adopted this to distinguish the two souls that live in me, the mask I wear (i) and my true face (I).*

Coming home never felt the same
A single death.
led the extinction
of a young soul.
High flight abandoned.

Tears hitting bathroom tiles
The slight echo of an empty room
blood spatter on a sidewalk in Hawaii,
the callous composition
of a contemptible piece of modern art

Sitting, cross-legged, on lonely rooftops
Walking through barren streets in a storm
Warmth escapes my fingertips
as winter air assaults my skin
She's depressed too but her laugh
is brighter than mine could ever be

The comfort of falling raindrops, camouflaging
The incomprehensible fleetingness of life
The mug that's now your memento
Your voice was unrefined honey with a touch of ginger
I miss your smile

and it haunts me

The flickering of street lamps as night settles
Wandering through hollow woods
Dreams unheard no longer matter

They always say I need to be strong
so I haven't followed...but
coming home

has never felt the same

<u>Lost after Paris</u>

The fragrance of lavender and
daisies drifting
through the winds of my memory

Dust on the keys of that grand piano, small notes echoing
as my foot presses down on the pedal
Fingers trace after the childhood i've begged not to lose
i desperately need to take shelter in it now

The past is a photograph that's never changed
i'm alone in a city
of suicidal thoughts
built by someone who claims
to be no one

I try desperately to forgive the unforgivable,
so that the unforgiving
Wont break me   so easily
like the vague strands of cindered cigarette smoke
That left my lungs bitter In remembrance
                    of the

Grace   and   Despair
                    of
                    our

                    tears

                    in

                    Paris

Guardian angel

Pour Papa

A dark angel slipped its silent hand in you
one night, without warning
You left for eternity
I was left
fatherless

the raindrops clouds shed are
tears, the gates of afterlife let escape
to find me
part of me wants to believe that
you're
somewhere
above us

Do you watch over me

from a realm beyond my understanding?
Then you would've seen me, beside your grave...
a child asking why
Daddy's eyes haven't opened since last night

She misses you
more than words could ever hope
to show you
She's been strong since you left, and I... I've tried
to emulate your light

They tell me I've inherited
your pen and your crown
They say I'm your spitting image
When you watch me now, do you see a pale reflection
do you see your eyes, weighed with deeper sadness?

7

My words ignite like budding flames from the impass-
ioned sparks of your living memory
The darkening blue of bruised flames, searing
grief onto parched paper, thirsting for a
Catharsis. My poetry
is your legacy
the only thing I have left
of you, to keep me whole

I'll find you again, once I've grown wings
but while bound to this world, I promise
I'll make you gleam with pride
So continue to watch over me
my angelic guardian

<u>All I have to do is remember her smile</u>

For Norma Anderson

It wasn't a funeral, I was told
it was a celebration of life

She was in more pain than any of us
but greeted us all with a smile
that never felt like mourning
Never hollowed out. she loved him
beyond existence
and I couldn't smile for her that day

I couldn't smile
I can't smile
I don't smile
I don't remember how to
smile

i just   divorce my lips, let my teeth
reflect sunlight, hoping it'll distract
from the swelling shadows trying to hide
underneath my eyes.

But, when I need to face the world
I remember her smile that day

9

Empty space

In 4th grade when I learned that atoms
were the building blocks of existence
I did not question it

I had never prayed to a god
                or a man   named adam

            I learned when I was eight, after I
finally understood why my father would never
wake up again,

          that faith was wishful thinking

In 10th grade when I learned that atoms
were mostly made up of empty space
I was not surprised

I had begun to understand my own existence
already beginning to unravel

         the meaning, within the melting
curves of my fingerprints,

       I had looked into the warmth

of shadows, between the comfortable
nook of my ribcage

        and found that it was mostly

Empty
space

11

In your passing

I found idle comfort
in dazed darkness
What was I to be
without the warmth
of your smile

Grief and Melancholy
offered me forever
so I gave them everything
I had left

But your soul still
lives on, in our memories
it pulls me into your light
whispering to me…

Don't give up,
you have so much to live for

Night colored wings

Blue lights feed off black nightmares

I was born from this nation's
infertile womb
You make me take an oath, a non-secular
prayer to your god in disguise

Hand over my heart
do I love this country?
            I plead the 5th.

How can I love
land within an imaginary border
What does it mean

to be a citizen
of this great white
nation, that seems to crave black blood
Gets a taste and goes into a frenzy
Of sirens, blinking lights and
gunshots   denying
freedom and culpability

What does it mean to be a part
of this well-oiled machine that runs
on the emptied marrow of breaking backs
And the indenturement of white-washed outsiders
i'd rather be apart from all of it
But I belong to the partisan chaos and I won't
run from the blue lights

Black Boy, Ebony Wings

Withered wings, chained
He stares at stars
dreaming of open flight, baptized
in luminescent moonlight.
Only dreams.
His ebony skin is a weapon used
to subdue him into submission

In this world where deathly pale,
alabaster reigns
white beady eyes, like cottonseed, only see
savagery, when looking down
on him. In this world his worth is not recognized

Everyday his eyes curve up towards the sky
his head is forced down
He's told he wasn't born the right
color   to fly
The flames of his passion flicker
down to their last embers. He stops dreaming,
Stops looking up towards freedom,
stops hoping...

But when the shouting sun's ultraviolet allure
soaks into his skin
He finds it is impossible to avert
his eyes, from the bewitching, blue sky

Warmth of sunlight,
soft clouds, untethered freedom
Temptations worth the risks of marching
a tight rope
hanging.   Strangled suffocation

of an imprisoned seeking liberation
He feels caged

by this inhospitable land, that never belonged to him.
His charred lineage first sailed across ravenous waters
under ivory boats, shipping promised
flesh confused for property rights.
The high ebbing tide separates him
from ravaged Elysian fields beneath black sun;
stolen kingdoms he should call home.

His chains, only nourished by his own polluted
thoughts they corrupted
It was his mind that was shackled
Night colored feathers cannot be tamed
The sky, above unforgiving soil,
is where he belongs
He owns the strength to change
his reality

He unfurls wings, black as starless skies,
black as lustrous skin
and soars into the night,
floating freely, on emancipated winds

Fierté Africaine

Pour ma famille

Je suis fier
de mes racines noires
comme ma mère m'a appris

J'adore comment l'humidité, des saisons des pluies,
est absorbé entre les brins enroulés de mes
cheveux noirs et crépus
J'adore la lueur brillante de la peau ébène
sous notre soleil rayonnant,
alimentée des années de beurre de karité

J'adore le retour au Bénin,
En atterrissant, l'air adopte le parfum des épices
un souvenir de l'huile de palme
J'adore nos cérémonies de baptêmes des nouveaux-nés
et la sagesse de la divination d'Ifa
J'adore nos Aso-oke traditionnels et la musicalité de Yoruba
J'aime ma negritude
et comment, quand tu me regardes, tu peux goûter

la douceur amère du chocolat noir,
à travers les champs nus de ta langue,
comment tu peux sentir le rythm d'un tambour
dans mes pas
et entendre une joie musical, amplifiée
dans mes lèvres pleines

J'adore que même quand je me serais effacé de ce monde,
mon corps, décomposé,
vous déchiffrez toujours, a travers mes os,
que je suis né d'un sang Africain et d'une terre noire

African pride

For my family

I am proud
of my black roots
as my mother taught me

I love how the humidity of rainy seasons
gets trapped between the curled strands of my
black, nappy hair
I love how lustrously ebony skin glistens
beneath our loving sun
from years of lathered shea butter

I love the flight back to Benin,
As we land, the air adopts the fragrance of spices
reminiscent of palm oil
I love our naming ceremonies and the wisdom of Ifà
I love our traditional Aso-oke and the musicality of Yoruba
I love my blackness
and how, when you look at me, you can taste

the bittersweetness of dark chocolate, dancing
across the bare fields of your tongue,
how you can feel the beat of a drum in my footstep
and hear the simple joy of music swell from my full lips

I love that even when i've faded from this world,
my body decomposed,
you'll still be able to tell, from my bones
That I was born of African blood and black soil

Poem for Parkland

_For every victim of
mass shootings, and
every grieving family_

Bullets flew
slicing loudly through air, like swallows singing
of the end.
Bullets pierced
through parting flesh like water
17 never made it
out the door.
17 juvenescent hearts ceased beating.
17 moments of silence

We march for them, in weary indignation,
vowing to slay violence with peaceful protest

When our leader heard of the gunshots, heard of
the bodies, hitting freshly scuffed floor tiles,
they began dissecting the issue, before the autopsies
had even begun, declaring it an issue of mental illness,
clinging to their unrelenting denial

Politicians speak a different language than we do
They claim not to understand ours—a dialect of swift action
Too much blood money crawling down their throats,
to speak anything other than conflict of interest

But have *them* watch their own children fall,
like wingless angels,
splayed over the ground
Have *them* hold their own child's lifeless body
embedded with enough bullets
to write out an elegy

Have them frozen in that moment
when their first tears attempt to escape

        They'll be fluent
        in our tongue by morning

Black wallflowers don't blend

Our ancestral tongue is a symphony of notes
$\qquad\qquad$ I never learned how to play.
Your voice in our village is a foreign beauty,
a death signal
for my umbilical connection
$\qquad\qquad$ to the land I should belong to

Western ideals demand that I $\qquad$ [CONFORM]

$\qquad\qquad$ attempt to consume my
fractured
$\qquad\qquad$ lineage, and all $\quad$ my color $\quad$ (I must

$\qquad$ **blend**

in, with white backgrounds) $\qquad$ like a black wallflower

but black wallflowers can't $\quad$ **blend** $\quad$ or be bleached

$\qquad\qquad$ Red and white fingers crawled down

$\qquad\qquad$ my throat $\quad$ and ripped the black tongue

$\qquad\qquad\qquad$ from my swelling mouth

memories of my childhood, spilling

from severed heritage

$\qquad\qquad$ How can I pray, for america
$\qquad\qquad\qquad$ when we don't praise

the same gods.

Black heretics don't **Blend** We kneel before anthems with

our fist up

Our Bond

For mom

Across time
across dimensions
my love will reach you.
I was born into your arms
you were the first to hold me.
Unquantifiable
the bond we share

Stunning temptress

Man-made neon lights

Lost
in self-destructive
chaos.   Falling
like unexpected rain
on days you thought were sunny

i pursue the fading,
northern sky constellations, swirling
around my entropic mind
Though they may have been nothing
more than man-made neon lights
guiding me in the wrong direction

My lonely hand, quick to reach
out, like strands of moonlight,
reaching   for lonely howls
Neon lights taunted, showing me where i'd hear
their songs of devotion. I've never grasped
the attainable. I've trod carelessly, through
the sanctity of pious desires

Reaching
Reaching
Reaching

Neon lights sung to me of wolves,
that were just as starved

We are only flawed

After Morgan Parker

River winding waist, eroded hips like
Smoothed ocean rock
Can desire emasculate?
Then I've encased myself in a woman's skin

I've always found myself effeminate, so I am at war
with the patriarchal oppressor in myself.

I was told to always treat women
as well as I would myself
So I end up treating them like they'll never be
good enough
Because we're self-destructive and only the sky knows
that there's a pin in us; clench your teeth around it and pull
Watch the parts of us you thought beautiful disassemble

I'm told I should smile more often
because It gives my face radiance
I can feel their tongues on my teeth.
I want to say this face is griefs masterpiece
but refuse to have my trauma mislabeled again
So I say: this is my resting bitch face and she smiles
for no one.
Find her in prayer, half begging
her teeth to fall out with a smile she offers
to no one.

You don't know my smile
How it howls.
Telling itself it'll never be enough
You haven't seen the missing wrinkles at the edges

You haven't felt the rot buried beneath my cavities
My mouth decays behind the golden drip of daylight

I want to be flawed like for once we are only human

And own a flawed Love that tries
to embrace how broken we've become
        And when I say broken I mean
So used to not being loved right or loved enough
That we've begun to settle for just any flawed love

Lost in our interstellar

Your mind is a galaxy, brimming
full of wandering stardust
The universe, a paradox, lost
in your milky brown eyes
Your dark matter   indefinite.
Take me

past the sublime threshold
of our known universe.
we'll tread upon the fading
sanctity of space,
like iridescent comets aflame
questioning life and
taunting death.
*****

You and I
have been quantumly entangled
since the birth of bleeding suns
        since the beginning
                of eternity
with time until infinity, to eventually slip
between the empty space of our atoms
        We vibe in unison
Unknown to ourselves and each other

We are stellar remnants
****

Celestial memories
of supernovas
We are two, merging, neutron stars;
                our collision

exuding gravitational waves
tremors   through space-time fabric

The exotic patience of our planetary distance

Every particle of my cosmic body spins
        around your angular momentum
Intertwinement   of our magnetic
coalescence
Your heartbeat pulses nebulae winds
The relics

of your luminous core
radiating midnight rays, only visible
to the dark-adapted.

Polarized flux
of our interstellar defiance;
our faint traces of light
lost, in our

singularity

The girl I met in April

The first sonata April composed
was of her sunlit,
hazel eyes... so stunning
I dare not gaze
too deeply into them
With a radiant smile more divine
than Nirvana's promise
inevitably I was drawn to her;
With every sigh she breathed
every smile her lips revealed
the world around me illuminated
She became my muse,
Her Spring morning melody
She became my poetry

Sweet disaster

Her favorite colour is my hysteria
but still I imagine
her lips would be my favorite getaway
A sweet disaster
like sudden meet-cutes, when
lost fragments of worn-out lovers
collide, accidentally
trading pieces of each other
filling in all the wrong empty spaces

Blank canvas

A blank canvas, she
would take on whatever colors
you dared paint her with
I found her, floating,
a transient beauty
Dazed eyes, trapped
in a dream-like
trance,   drifting

her eyes met mine, unfocused
an aching smile etched across her visage, pale
translucent skin like the clouds she spent her days
gazing at, seeming almost serene,
in her faded sundress
Was it really alright
for me to shake her
from this dream?

I wanted to take her
to where calming skies turn to ash
Corrupted
cries of man replacing silent winds
Velvet tears staining
her soul, consumed by a decaying world
I wanted her
tainted
by the kind of knowledge
that erodes sound sleep

Who says truth is beauty   after all

But I left her   with the clouds
unable to paint her with the shadows

that haunt my wilting
soul

The dancer

So graceful she seemed to levitate
taming gravity as she
soared across stages
entrancing her audience with the way
her body moved in fluid motion
her steps, elegant yet fierce
In moments, I was on my knees
She was passion's embodiment

i captured the world through my lens,
fleeting moments frozen in time,
But i could never capture
Her
She was freedom

the fates guided her summer wind to find me
and we danced over black swan lakes
Traced the surface, leaving behind
our spirits' echoes, to ripple across the waters

I won't be addicted to our sunlight

Your gravity is intense
        Your sweetness is
    Addictive
Like drugs and candy
        You have those powers
        over me
            planetary pull
You might strangle me
        with desire
My hot breath
        something you do
    to me
You have those powers
        Over me
            Like moon to
    an evening primose

I wanted to watch
        You bloom while
            I withered in
        Sourceless sufferance
and I asked
        Beautiful, what is left
            of us
Maybe we're just
defective

        I let your heart
        fall
so carelessly
        Through the cracks of
            my hands, split from
emotional earthquakes

It was you
who taught me how to run
It was I, who taught you
that you were
nothing
but a ghost
without a voice
I ran from you,
like mercury
with winged feet,
To where only gods
could take the flightless

My arms still fit
through the holes of your
Baggy sweater, faded green like
dying pine trees
and those poems are only
alive when I'm not

i was born in the clouds
But you ground me
As if you can make
sullen clouds, grey like athena's eyes,
shed me like raindrops
I couldn't be yours
For weeks or years
Because I was terrified
Of being addicted to sunlight
When I should be
Accustoming myself
To the darkness
I lied and said was beautiful

Poems to my beloved

The silence in her eyes

It's in your eyes that I find myself
reflected
It's in your eyes that I find a sacred truth
i can only describe as beauty
and It's in your eyes
That i've found what lies between the silence
of my uncertain love and your knowing touch

I find myself unable to deny that my poetry
was born to define what's been left unsaid.

In your eyes I found, a hidden voice
that sings quietly, with nightingales, the sorrows of memory
A song I knew by heart.
We've both known   unknowingly,
since the first unspoken whisper between our eyes,
that we both sing our melancholy in the same tongue-
A mute melody whose refrain only resonates
between the two of us

Lovers destiny

i can no longer ignore the loud beating
of my heart, trying to break
free from its cage of hardened marrow,
when i imagine how soft your lips would be
against mine.
But oceans were placed between us
by delicate divine hands, and *Eshu*[2] whispered to me

That i should not yearn for you

Am I alone in feeling the universe toy with my love?
a love I bury every night.
i should not sail through vast crystalline waters
just to hold you, with desire strong enough to brittle steel
only fools let love lead them
We were never meant to be felt, like wildfires
self-consumed

Fade my name from your lips
Remember me faceless, and forget
our spilling passions, like the white thread
that led us nowhere

Unless
you want to combat our destiny,
resow our fate in red thread,
then i'd be willing to tame the heavens
and take up arms

---

[2] *Eshu (Èṣù), is an Orisha, or West African deity (specifically of the Fon and Yoruba people) he is the divine messenger and the opener of different roads of life (his sign is the crossroads). He is also known as the trickster god*

against the gods themselves

Winter angel

in autumn's quiet demise
still hiding
inside myself
I swear off love,
My fractured fingers, clawing
at the very walls I had erected

Her sunlight trickled faintly
through dense walls
makes me   smile
so effortlessly
like nothing else
New colors overflow from me
attraction flourishing, like budding
roses through thorns

She appeared, descending into my arms
like a winter angel
And I embraced my new *raison d'etre*
For how could I live without love

She was my world and I spun around her
orbit, like debris from a crumbling moon
finding a home in her planetary rings,
both of us ignoring the wreckage
that still followed the other

Why we don't do I love you's anymore

When I tell you I love you
I get frustrated
How could those three empty words
ever do this feeling justice
and sometimes I think you'll never understand what I mean
I'm not sure I ever will either
But that is the most powerful expression
I know of. My mouth is a canyon and those words are
diluted when slipping from the river of my tongue
because I've said love like it was a greeting
to any passing stranger who locked eyes with me
I've said beauty as if every one of us
holds the soul of a saint inside ourselves
I've said I love you like it was a curse
I've said I love you like it was a blessing
I've said I love you like it meant nothing
I've said I love you like the words were music to your ears
but never mine
I've said I love you like the words were clad in black armor
I've said I love you like it could save us
like it was our salvation
like the absence of those haunting words
was our damnation
I said I love you but still can't understand
the different parts that comprise this promise
Can't understand the gears that make it turn
I've said I love you but
I've yet to know myself
I've never understood the dimensions of love
I've never truly felt you
And we've yet to understand *Us*
the *you* and *me* we've constructed in ourselves of each other
But what else am I to say in your presence

49

I was named 'devotion' in a past life

After Rudy Francisco

Maybe it's true
        that I love you only
because I need to feel loved
        by someone else, so I can convince
myself that I'm worth being loved.
        Maybe when you said we were kindred
souls, fated to last,   I was the one
            weaving our golden thread
        Maybe I chameleoned my way into your
heart.

Maybe when vulnerability peaked through
       your saddened flesh   I saw   devotion, in the way you

           could use me to sedate your sorrows.

Maybe when I say love you   I mean I find my self-worth
        in the way you smile when I offer you three
holy
prayers,
      like offering myself to god as an act of worship;
knowing that in me there's a desire strong
enough that i'd offer half of myself   to claim my other
half.

all for Love
     all for Love
all for Eden   all for Eve,   all for the death
of loneliness and the love   of serpents and the forbidden

Robin

For the nightingale who knew me

The nightingale sings like marigolds refusing praises
from the sun
I find it beautiful how our truth renders this as meaningless
as the vastness of a mostly empty cosmos

I pretend not to hear its song, only see
the bleeding rouge
of its chest feathers
Nightingales in silence
are often confused for robins
who own no music in them

The song that never belonged to me,
that's why i'll let blood
be the final word off my tongue—an apology
In its own way

The nightingale knits its song through skybound trees
nestles its melody in their trunk, so when the winds
grow violent
It'll find its way back home
Never offers a longing song in mourning
for a moon in phases
Distance only measurable
in skies that only ever seem to change, but never do
Moonlight duets are a myth, lunar light

only travels
in waves of inconsistency, offers itself
And only for the damned. The most starved
will wait for the impassioned fullness of a blood moon

Those with wings will see, it's just a strange shade
of a darker bruised blue

The Chaos of Pursuit

Was it not icarus who flew with wings too weak
to withstand the sun's splendor

We don't know where we belong

god gave us everything
She left   before telling us where we
belonged.
Left us lonely like muted letters in a mouthful of words

I partitioned my soul into the different aspects of our
misunderstanding
Edged body parts into a still
rotting   corpse
Dead   in another realm
        Dead here, a woman, of only silent
        words with unpronounced vowels

I watch myself from the sidelines
belonging to no one
make myself into a road—The final destination: to become
anyone other than who i've failed to be
Break the bonds with who i was or who i am
no longer trying to re:become
I want to forget
When my tracks are the only ones left in the snow, I still find
Yours   and I swallow my syllables so as not to rebirth you
We are the antithesis of beauty as a way to form identity
Like snowflakes or words that broke in our throats, we fall
Silent
i look above the snow tracks to remember
There's a slow-moving galaxy in the unique uniformity
of snowfall

My life's pursuit

I spent my life chasing her
How long has it been now?
How long have I sought her
How long has her very essence enticed
every ounce of my being?
Yet never a step closer do I seem
My heart and soul still ache for her
Her name is Love,
Her name is Freedom,
Her name is joy

Fated Flight

After John Magee's "High Flight"

Fly with me on the clouded canvas
Caressed by the sun's warm glow
Chase the laughing wind in sun-split silence
under the blue canopy where heaven and earth meet
Beyond, where humanity's touch has not yet reached
Is where fate will take us
Where we will see and do a thousand things
we've never dared dream of
together, our fingers laced in each other's,
let's climb up empty footsteps
of saintly sky
and look down upon god's fallen kingdom
as we traverse through the unsung sanctuaries
of distant, unsullied paradises

I hope our paths cross again

These days I still catch your afterimage
in the corners of my eye,
I cannot pry your influence from my mind
Your name remains
tattooed on the inside of my eyelids
so you'll stay forever in my dreams
Perhaps fate will have us cross paths again
and erase our past
Just enough for us to start over

Nowhere Origins
The winds had seen bodies sick, with viridescent flesh
slowly gripping stiff and brittle bones
not ashes
but ashes in time

I am from nowhere

i've found myself
stitched into nameless roads to
forgotten memories

I am from nowhere
i was born before ashes
I was born before the memories
conceptualized with hopes before my body had felt light

My soul carries a map to itself, keeps it close
On it, every destination that ever held me

Atlanta's hospital stands on a secluded island
of intricately cobwebbed picture frames
Atlanta was my amnesia paradise of splintered frames

Takoma is my center sanctuary
Takoma is a two-bedroom apartment that anchored me.
Takoma is where I felt weightless, before
tempting skies and seductive, glinting edges

Sligo Creek elementary stands next to P.S. 96, the grim
filthiness of New York staining Silver Spring's sun
Paris is summer and second homes through clouds
Paris is my tenth birthday when snow angels smiled
like they already knew the surprise waiting for me

61

Congo was not always in my heart, I learned to love it
I grew into its sun until blood diamonds could
drink my grief, for all the women who never
had a chance to thrive in its light

The soil of Africa was different from america
humid and dry seasons filled my lungs with meaning
Benin and Cameroon were the difference between
the starkness of clouded mountaintops and the muddled
ambiguity of seas near nostalgic shores I seek

I was born before black stained soil
i was born before black bodies dropped
I am from nowhere

my skin carries a weight I cannot
fathom when I am alone
but my name is a revolution I wear like a crown

I've never sought to bleach away Africa from my veins
Though I longed for my oppressors in her womb
and now, i've never missed her more... apprehensively.

A mothers dust clings
to my pores
the way I tried so desperately
to cling to   anything.

I am from nowhere
I was molded through tears
i was born in the space between
bodies and ashes

One step forward

If I had the strength to split dark
clouds and let light peer through
I wouldn't be here telling you
I'm not the man I hoped to be
I can't bear to show you
That i'm not capable
Of casting away the moon to let night die
This somber sky is merciless and leaves no space
for moons that empty themselves everyday
from the fullness of bright suns

But he's waiting

i chase after him fervently
legs moving faster than wind
The gap never closes
This long, daunting road
never shrinks.
The man I'm meant to be
is waiting
though if I see time as my ally
and not my foe
Then slowly, one patient step at a time
I'll reach him

Pursuit of intimacy

I want to love
somebody like you
I want to know all of you
I've never felt true intimacy
Its smooth magma slowly dripping
down my callow lungs
Come closer

I want to see in your eyes
this feeling i've only witnessed
in the aftermath of a poet's pen
i want the first taste

of a vanishing star
and your lascivious lust
as you drink from the emerald chalice
of my chastity.
Savor the falling waters

of my desire's melting glacier
Undress my mind and let me rest
my eyes on the wonders lost
beneath you
i want you
to find in me what's never been seen.
I've never been felt behind my smile.

Let me sink in your hidden sadness, feel the raw
heat of your wild, silent embers
and drown in our growing passion

Chasing sunrises

"A beautiful confusion... The story of a boy who chased sunsets, until they chased him"

—*Syre*

The boy chased sunrises
not realizing he was sinking
into the sea with the dipping sun

The boy was fearless
until he came face to face with
His own smiling shadow and its desires

The boy's words were beautiful
until he wrote his truth

The boy who thought he had died
found his pulse in poetry

Ask me one more time

One more time
ask me
if I'm alright
and when i lie
berate me   again   and   again
with kind words and compassion
until my walls crumble
with the false strength i've worn for years
Watch as I break and
hold me up as I tell you softly of my suffering
I can no longer bear to fall on my knees.
You'll read in my begging eyes,
that paint my yearning for intimacy,
A tale of sorrow

Part.2: Eclipse

Hell:(n)
/hel/
Origin- Germanic (hölle-hel-hell)
Indo-European root, meaning
"To cover or hide"

Fall from grace

Fall from grace

A soul, lost
Fall from grace
withered wings
like a black hole
absorb all light
Leaving nothing but
Despair

Dual singularity horizons

how many/of the stars tonight are/man-made/planes
masquerading as celestials/nothing ethereal/about our ungodly/
bodies/ broken/
/torn/abandoned/self-immolate
in our insecurities/our bodies/only vessels/let me escape/let me
glow like fireflies/in unsullied/open fields/still, I offer strangers/
my bleeding/heart/ hoping for shelter/home/was meant to be
in me/I was meant to cherish/inner temples/not pray
at the feet/of passing/lovers—
Black sun   White noise
   Empty home.
Burnt to the ground. We're all bleeding
      into temporary palms.
     Homeless. Escape from
 Home into where you can't be found
      Disappear

The idea of disappearing//My particles fade
   The beauty of hollowing
out your shadow/to make space for yourself/
you are no one/disappear disappear/until you are
   /nothing/understand
//The poetics of nonexistence//

our bodies and souls were made eons ago
when we were singular. Beings
we were once simple attraction repulsion
Do you not see why our souls are entangled
   and strangled by each other?
We were never impossible
maybe more probable than
The inevitable
Death of faith

After an admission of guilt
We wait for the right reasons to disappear
From each other   or in each other

Masks to hide a hostaged soul

A mask, worn
to hide
a soul taken hostage
by its own shadows.
Slow
suffocation

Wide smile, booming laughter,
the prancing jester has them all fooled
Silently begging for anyone
to see
The missing pieces in his facade, that let
teardrops fall unnoticed.
....
i don a frail impersonation
of a man i used to be
step into someone else's skin, camouflage
myself, with all the other unburdened smiles

laying on cold roof tiles
as I watch the soft glow of manmade stars
stream past me, I muse
of a soothing end, where
this body is returned to me

Permanent smile carved on my lips
My humanity peels
off, in shades of grey and artifice
Behind the disguise—a writhing heart
tormented by
a grating melody of rage and sorrow

Anxiety is a noose

Anxiety
is not a prison
Anxiety is a noose
ingrained in my mind like the roots of a giving tree
and on those days when I've mistaken myself for brave
I feel the chair fall from under me
my breath is stolen
and I feel the rope tighten around my heartbeat

My clumsy tongue, scarred by familiar words
that tumble around my mouth like broken
shards of shattered windows
I let the words fall
silent inside of me
and give them life in poems

I should feel comfortable around my friends
but my mind has convinced me
that little whispers are let loose from their
false smiling lips
and that every harrowing laugh in the distance
is about me   so I distance myself
Never trust them fully with what I am

I want to have fun but fun is terrifying and no longer
fun when I have to leave my bed
I'm overcome with guilt for not wanting
to interact yet I want so much to want it
Ma tells me to go see my friends and leave
my room once in awhile but the thing is
i'm not sure I have a single friend in the world
i have people i surround myself with
because i feel obligated to socialize

but their jagged smiles don't make me feel at home

Parties are a personal purgatory for me
i'm never quite sure what to do with my body
never know what to say
I become caught in a snake's nest
It coils around my organs and asphyxiates
        my ears, drumming from the vibrations
of a swarm of bees buzzing in my throat
We're talking to each other but not with each other
and your eyes are staring deeper than I can handle.

Every time I step outside I feel

like running
away
Every time I step outside
I can feel the hand of god reach
into my mouth
His fingers are thick they taste of salt and bitter ale
his fingernail scrapes the slimy film that coats my uvula
and I immediately
fall
to my knees
in defeat
crushed by how incapable I am

Anxiety is a noose

        I
    am the prison

and I won't step out
of myself again

so they'll never get to
see me
|
hang

I watched her as she left

I'm a man without a home
I watched her walk away
stood still as the sound of her footsteps grew softer
in the distance.
Now i wander an endless vacuum
searching for shelter in anyone but myself.
Our love was a sunset, our love was
the vanishing sun

I wish I could erase you

I was at your mercy,
you poured yourself deep in the burrows
of my lungs
I hate that I needed you
I lived and died only by your whim
my only source of oxygen

If I can't breathe without you then I'll plunge
into frozen waters and survive without air
If you were my paradise then I'll find peace
in the pits of purgatory

Never again will I be
at the mercy
of someone I once loved

The cup we drink from

After Khalil Gibran

Prelude—"You would drink love from a cup, but not from a
surging river"

You would
rather drink
Love from
a cup, than
from the
origin of its
pure flowing
river, because
you cannot
possess, nor
hold/contain
the flowing,
only the still

You tried to possess our self-contained love
Don't ever think you truly loved me
I was the idea of love you fell for
Not me, you never really
loved me.
but
we,
are
both guilty of this

On the brink

I've tasted the salt of my own tears
heard the infinite   echo
from the bowels of my misery
Everyone wants a taste of their inner paradise
but my joy is a myth

Existential hatred, directed
inward, eating away at a will to live
no helping hands resting on my shoulder
No one coming to my rescue
No one left

lost soul swallowed.
      the bitter-sweetness
swarming in bottomless chasms
leaves you
hollowed out, leaves you
constantly on the brink
 yet
      still barely breathing,
      Leaves you
         utterly

    Alone

Winds Untamed

Poetic cure

I carve poetry
Into bare flesh.
I crave it.
Poetry is
dopamine
inside my bloodstream
I inject ink
into my veins
like It's the cure to all
my demons

Lost words i cannot find

My feelings for you are lost
behind words
i may never find

All I know
is that I was your friend
always there
for you, but I felt my heart desire
more...

I find myself unable to meet your eyes
I am too bare within your palm
my soul, twisted somewhere between your fingers
It terrifies me
that I've given you the power
to break me
with a single
breath

When you see me in the halls

Do you too, feel that agonizing
ache, gripping your chest
when our eyes meet in the distance
Does it pain you
to look away and walk past me
without letting a single word
escape your lips
Or was I just a way to pass time
and this agony, mine alone to bear?
To you, am I only the fading
memories of our fractured sunlight?
Then soon I'll disappear

Distraction from the shadows.
As my eyelids find each other beneath the dimming sky,
what shapes my nightmares
is the

                    Emptiness

    That begs
dark thoughts
to leak out
from empty dimensions
parallel   my destruction

We hold each other
because we're afraid
of being alone
only love the lonely in each other
addicted to bleeding
into open arms

I know this shallow infatuation is nothing
more than a distraction
But i'll let myself be absorbed by her
until I can step out
of my soul entrapping shadows

You (you) and I (i) falling out of each other
I
We spoke with fluffed voices
Two hollowed out echoes reflecting
into each other, never saying much
but having so much to say
i couldn't ever whisper those hollow ringing words
into your ear, hoping they would reach you
Those deceptively beautiful words that can change
in wholeness like moons do
i won't ever let you know
how i wanted you to keep me closer than your heartbeat
that the distance between us made my body ache

II
There's a small daydream I fall into, even now,
whenever I find the clouds staring back,
in which my soul lies afloat in imagined gaiety
You and I share a smile, and your eyes, like mine,
betray who you've always been. And I follow
your laugh, like a hypnotizing tune, back to our home
where the two of us are still broken
but healing in each other
instead of falling apart in our desperation
to mean something
to each other

Decaying world,
only love can heal

Muslim in Alabaster kingdoms

The surly, dark-haired waitress stares at me
as I let my mother tongue slip smoothly from my lips
Daggers pierce me as I set my Arabic free in public,
my tongue curls confidently around familiarity
Hostility is no match for a taste of home

But I cannot ignore the contempt of nations
It tortures, out of view
in windowless dungeons
The hatred and fear of millions drain us of life.
We've been left to drown in our own
blood and unforgiving shame
The crimes of few will be paid with the lives of millions
and scars left on billions.
Bludgeon us with scorn, but know that you
have created what you fear

Bullets penetrate skulls, fear mongering
rhetoric perforates sound minds that wish no harm.
So painful... I might renounce my god
just to live in peace, I might renounce my god so you
may cease to fear me
back home apostasy is a death sentence,
There is nowhere left to go

Will there ever be a world
where we are all accepted as we are?

War's fallen justice

Those who drop bombs in the name of Justice
hide behind self-righteous masks
that thinly veil grotesque agendas
consumed by greed

Some wage holy wars,
scarring their own prophets
as blood flows on both sides

We are all one in death

god's tears cannot cleanse dirtied hands
There are no heroes or justice in war

We hand our soldiers a death sentence
send them off with death's scythe
Armed head to toe with their guns
and unmarked gravestones
The war ravaged lose everything, while
behind the scenes
Those at the top fill their pockets
with blood-spattered bills
Living in luxury, dining on the frigid corpses of the fallen

Our Rising Voices

After Maya Angelou

I   Jan 20th 2017

The clouds shed tears with millions of us today.
A truly surreal scene.
My voice is lost, this country has left me
speechless…
What have we done

I hear the mournful chant of sullen angels
Fallen glory of freedom fought for
We've let hungry, avaricious hands
slit the tender throat of our nation.
The graves of our ancestors shudder
under the weight of our mistakes

We cannot let our country be overtaken
by the intolerant souls that would ravage her

II   Jan 22nd 2017

Did you think you had broken us
with your rigged results
you've only brought us closer together
our strength, fortified, in the face of adversity
We are an ocean of color and a storm is coming
The blood of past civil triumphs runs
through our veins. We are the vision
of the immigrant, of the refugee, of the slave

You try to beat us into the ground, hoping we turn to dust
We rise up, unbroken
You try and obstruct our justice,
with fear, over-policing and lead bullets

We rise up, unbroken
You try and starve our spirits until our own deprived
palms, rescind our god-given rights,
while you hand us back the sails that brought us here,
We continue to rise up
unbroken
and history will tell our tale

Can you hear their voices
Somewhere, a soldier cries himself to sleep
but not for his fallen comrades
he weeps for the small child whose innocent
life he ended, with the single flick of his trembling
finger, on an unforgiving trigger
The same child who'll haunt his nights
when he's safe back home

Soldiers are used like expendable
pawns, taking bullets for politicians
who wouldn't sacrifice a paycheck
for those suffering
Lockheed sells, then
bodies pile. Payment,
for a war no one wanted
Stirring images in the media, of death and war,
are ignored as we go about our daily lives

The growing chorus of their beatless hearts
too quiet for us to take notice

Can't you hear their thundering
murmurs, from the clouds?
Still begging for mercy

Imagine

Imagine
you've been living in a body
That doesn't feel like yours
a rented vessel
Imagine the label you were slapped with
the day you were born
is slowly strangling you
You can't breathe,
You want to speak out, but you're choking
on words you can't set free
Society binds you to an identity you've tried so hard to reject
Every prescribed pronoun pierces you like cold steel
everyone sees you as something you're not
But who can blame them when you
reflect everything they've forced you to be
everything you've tried so desperately
to escape from

Imagine, when you finally strip
away that false body
and reveal yourself to the world
Society, repulsed, quickly smothers you
with that same label again, denying your identity

What hurts more than hateful slurs
or the looks, the whispers, the bruises
is the slow pain of cutting away at your own soul
as you desperately try and hide who you truly are

Religious zealots look down on you,
with sanctimonious
disdain, bibles aimed
shooting devout rhetoric like hollow-point bullets

100

You ask yourself: "Was it not your god who made me this way?"

Imagine you've been ostracized until
you no longer feel   human.
self-hatred gnawing at you from inside
you become numb
There's only one escape.

Imagine
at the edge,
as your fingers dance with the depraved notion of the end
something pulls you back;[3] A friendly smile
concerned eyes, a warmth you almost forgot—
Love

You are never alone

---

[3] ; "A semicolon is used when an author could've chosen to end their
sentence, but chose not to. The author is you and the sentence is your
life." - Project Semicolon, a movement dedicated to presenting hope.

The face of war

They enter in the night
Blood splatter graffitis town walls
smog masks moonlight
The putrid stench of burning flesh consumes the air
piercing cries echo like sirens

The sound of stomping boots sends vibration through your bones
You struggle to hear your mother shouting over gunfire
A hail of bullets bursts
from the wall, separating you
from the rest of your family
You crouch under a table, hear your little brother screaming
he's just a baby
The house crumbles along with your composure...
You've just narrowly escaped
now all you can do is
Run.

The scent of blood becomes all too familiar
with each step, A horrid opera of excruciating howls
envelops you as you watch body parts soar
You pass mutilated bodies, just barely recognizing some
The girl who sat next to you in class, the friendly baker
With the warm smile
No time to mourn, but their unblinking gazes have been
seared into your subconscious.

Loud explosion up ahead,
you're flung backwards
Pain courses through your body, the ground
comes crashing against your back
The last thing you remember is staring up at the sky
You can no longer see the stars amidst the chaos....

******

The dust clears and you search your house,
which once held your fondest memories, for any sign
of your family
The stench of death reigns above today, but you still have hope

You find your brother's limp, lifeless body
and as you hold him, tears overflowing,
your cries join the somber echo

The ones who invaded your home and slaughtered
innocent families
will turn to the world, wave their star spangled
propaganda and claim this was justice
Where is the justice in senseless murder?

Virtue has always been at the mercy of victors
Truth bends at the fingertips of conquerors
It seems compassion is only a geopolitical tool.
This is true human nature.

They'll never be held in chains for their war crimes.
Instead, you, who watched helplessly as they all died,
will be labeled a threat.

Your face tainted by the blood of your family,
sitting in the rubble of what used to be your world
You've lost everything
lost faith
in god
and in humanity

Today we are human

You and I were born with only love in our hearts
our differences are not a divide
they should only embolden us
Today I am not
gay, straight, black, bisexual, american, african, atheist,
transgender, christian, muslim, man or woman
Today I am human
Let's break down these borders
Tear down these imaginary walls
let my compassion touch your soul
let's welcome each other with open arms
for this earth is both mine and yours

Scarred feathers

At your wake

Pour mami

My fingers traced the flesh
in the hollow of your cheek
only then did my heart believe
what my ears could not,
that you had truly left us
left us with a lifeless smile
left us to mourn
in bittersweet reminiscence.
They told me not to cry
I could not follow those simple orders.
They told me many things I could not hear
frozen in the moment I first saw you in your stillness
They all told me
that you're in a better place now
Is there such a place better than by your family's side?
Maybe they're right
Maybe this world is sufferance
Maybe this world never deserved you
to begin with

Suns collapsed

Suns collapsing
Stars swoon in Spring skies
As if Autumn's passing was only the dawn
of our new days
Suns collapsing, tunneled vision.
Hear the sirens howl through playful winds
as if Kalypso never warned us
Suns collapsing, imperfect implosions.
Light traces every being. Brittle frost shrouds
flower petals floating off after high noon
above light, like the ashes of mankind
Suns collapse. Leaving only
the dim decay of darkening daylight

Flood

My eyes are a dam
with walls made from hollow hymns
            I sung so sorrowfully to myself, in that
lonely church without windows.
            The walls melt away
like iron in the core of a dying star
                    when I think about how
        you left this earth so soon

I am flooded

I could be loved

*"To be hurt, wounded and
punished by your
own understanding of love
and then bleed willingly"*
— Khalil Gibran

As long as I change for *them*
after sowing closed the fresh, gaping
wounds, left behind in me,
As long as they don't pull at the stitches
watching my scars bleed like holy prayers as they
Sink their teeth into my unraveling flesh

Then I can be loved too

That is what my heart spoke to me
so worthlessly
I am the dry *desert rose* he'll try and press
between two pages
I am the cracked canvas she'll paint over
with colors so dark you'll no longer find
a single flaw

But I can't go back
to abandoning myself to the anaesthetics
of emotionless numbing
can't shape myself with softer edges, just so the wrong
lover can hold me
Only love's tender cruelty can shape
my understanding
The pain of broken hearts
is a gift

I bleed willingly

and it feels sweeter now
than the safety of

                              numbness

Beautiful stranger do not fall

"I turned you into a stranger
in order to forget you"
— Carlos Ruiz Zafón

Beautiful stranger gazing longingly at me
with eyes that shapeshift color
like sunlight through a teardrop
I notice every fleck in the pattern
of his iris. He's begun to fall
for a mask
                I blame myself

I ignored the subtle melodies of my heart
but in my poetry I am bare, my raw
mind reared open.

Beautiful stranger, do not fall
for me, I am lost behind
closeted insecurities, so hidden
you'd have to dig through concealed flesh,
deep in the space beneath inner scar tissue,
Just to find me

you cannot fall, as I have fallen,
there are growing   rifts
between the cracks in my mask, i cannot bear
for you to see—the closer you look
the more solemn seems my smile

So, stunning stranger
whose touch is still unknown to me,
do not fall

I beg of you

Fallen Saviours

Without me in your way

I've been told my voice isn't as strong or as loud
as all the other poets.
I think of my father's voice.
How it has faded but still holds on to its willpower.

I can't scream my pain into the void of a stranger's ears
unless I'm in a locked room.
I wonder what kind of power a whisper can hold
My voice is less than unspoken,
it's a graveyard. dead weight hanging
inside my throat.

The most beautiful moment in my life was when
a woman on a train whispered
thanked me as I got out of her way
No one ever thanks me for getting out of their way
I squeeze every drop of night into my own iris and cut myself
out from their lives, surgically removing myself
for their own safety, or maybe
I just didn't want to be there to watch
them self-immolate for their belief
that trauma has made us broken and healing is the only
prayer god chooses to ignore.

Last year when I looked into the mirror, broke off the blade
from my razor kit and with the quivering veins of my left arm,
gave the bathroom tiles a fresh coat of paint—The mirror man
never thanked me
for getting out of our way

Savior complex

i was the black knight
meant to save the princess trapped in her tower
But as i gazed upon that daunting edifice
i was left to wonder, if i could ever truly save a lost soul,
from white-winged demons of melancholy and withdrawal
Yet, i continued to strike with my sword
of empty promises, to no avail

As the morning star slipped away and night settled
i layed restless under the crescent moon
seeing flashes of her pass me by
Her once passionate eyes, bereft of hope
losing their light that once loved. Though,
from her stoic features, newly hardened by
tragedy, i had found
an enigmatic beauty in her inconsolable eyes,
to which her silence added layers

Strange how tragedy can be so beautiful

She never reached for my outstretched hand,
ignoring my weightless words, muffled
through the dulled mouthpiece of
my masculinity-(savior) complex
muting my intentions

Still, I ran in place,
chasing her
unmoving tower, trying to save
myself
through her

My head, fighting temptations of

abandonment
I made a promise
to myself, that I'd always be there to save her
if only with my powerless
words.
******

I've always known that you
don't need me
to save you.
You are stronger than I could ever
hope to be, in ironclad armor
but you are my
hope
So give me a sign
that things are better;

My one regret

Two strangers carrying shards
of shared memories
A past
once graced by compassion
You were my one

regret
Letting you go or having
met you, I do not know.

A silent tear blurs my vision, rendering my writing muddled
As I write of you, I feel
ethereal fingers wrap
around my heartbeat, tightening
As I long for you
my words escape along clouds, out of reach
they linger across smooth feathers in flight, leaving me empty
The ink refuses to stitch along the starving page
My voice is a muted prayer, caught

in my chest
My heart holds on to it, unwilling
to let me say the thousands of things
I've always wanted to tell you
My mind consumed by you—a drowned body.

Struggling to move forward,
I trudge through high tides
staring back at you, as waves crash against me
Tempted to pursue the precious memory of you still

Ode to the romanticization of Death

After José Saramago

O' Death, your beauty has not yet been seen
by all those who tremble at your mere name

We need you as night needs moon
so morose night's reign would be without moonlight
So too would we be without your embrace

You are cruel to those you've stolen from
but mustn't we all head for that light someday?
If not for you, Death, there would be
no end to illness or war
no end to the torment
that life inflicts
Is it not Life we should fear instead
and the agony He engraves
deep into the flesh of our existence

Death, you are
humanity's savior

Life wraps his coarse hands around our fragile necks
slowly mangling our decrepit bodies
Only with your sweet kiss, Death, will we find everlasting
serenity
You offer our pitiful souls a gentle escape.

But Death, you are frightful.
In absence of sunlight, your name is a welcomed solace
But for those who've danced with time
and know their waltz will soon end at any moment
For those who've felt your gaze and your cold
touch, linger gingerly along goosebumped flesh

121

Who've seen your aftermath, trailing
behind our tail, stealing those closest to us
To those of us who know you
You are ferocious, You are destruction,

You are sorrow

Apokalypse

final destruction - book of Revelation

/ə ˈpäkə ˌlips/

*Greek root - Apokaluptein-
"To Uncover, Reveal"*

Horsemen
Four brought my soul to apokalypse
My heart pumped stygian liquid
through sordid veins, in anguish
from woeful memories
they left engraved into my being
Love is a lie
Love is sufferance
Love is revelation

War

Hope's dying light clung
like winters last autumn leaves
and you were
the gentle wind that nurtured
my atrophying heart
with empty promises.

Living our loveless lie
mesmerized by the fickle phantasm
of what we thought love could be
until you were satisfied
and i was cast aside

No longer intoxicated by our frailty,
our hollow, conditional love,
I began discovering
the lost empires beneath my hidden sunlight

You taught me Love should never be a prison

Pestilence

We met through shared passion
Our hearts both bled ink and we wove
a similar sorrow with our black-feathered pens
i was infatuated by you
i was drifting through you

Dipping into love's shallow ends was enough
to find that it still carried the same depth and beauty
even after breaking me
But you and i were only passionate throes

and passion is ephemeral,
as my love for you, was like the cold light
of paling fireflies.
Bioluminescence glowing
flickering, between certainty and
uncertainty
until the very last moment
when light dissipates
finding its way up to the catacombs
of celestial divinity

You taught me love is never temporary

Famine

You and i were nothing more than
pillow talk and empty dreams
never kitchen floor plans or 401Ks
with thoughts of retirement homes in Panama
near the shore
You and i were monday morning regrets, written
on crumpled paper for the sun to burn away
You and i were a story with only one chapter
but no ending in sight
Never 9-5 struggles, never hand holding through rain
or reassurance, that everything would be ok
We were summer breakup amnesia
and unresolved passions/insecurities
We were drunk road trips under bed sheets

We were
Never I love you's

but i fell to that careless temptation,
chasing those words that could never belong to me
inhaling all your misery
Just to hold you deeper inside me
Eventually you told me i was yours, only
to ease the void left by a lost lover
told me now a stranger is all you wanted
me to be. You ended our story, before I had ever
truly felt you, our bodies had always been too blue
like passing moons and our poetics

Every poet will get caught chasing Love
We can't stay away even when we know
she's not real.
She'll crucify us

and we'll bleed joyously for her
time and time again

You taught me to be careful where I search for love

Death

Your eyes are forever
the birthplace of my poetry
I adopted your heartache
stained blank pages with my tears
disguised as yours

We pushed and pulled away
something always bringing me back
to your name

your slightly crooked smile, beneath
the teasing curl of your knowing lips
and the way you used to look at me
stole my breath
I would almost tremble
Unable to contain how much I needed you

I could feel myself
falling
through our eternity
falling
like love and other fantasies off my impatient tongue
falling
for...
a dream

Our words were too weak
and too powerful
to ever say anything meaningful
Now every time i try to write you into poems
I watch you fade off white paper
Immortalized in ink
but no longer immortal in me

I hope you find what ive never been
able to tell you, in the silence
of my absence

You taught me that love never learns

Tortured angel

The night's too long
When will daybreak arrive?
Brooding clouds swarm above me,
storms rage   pitch-black night
as endless as desserts
I wake, never to dawn

I awake, knowing
I'll be staring at
the same
somber
scene.

Moonlight once brought tranquility
to this infinite prelude
to twilight's first crack
but stole the few dwindling
stars, I held onto as she left

Still no sunrise.
will the light of day
continue to elude me?

Listless, I try and find idle serenity
In burning black skies
that seem almost
poetic

The darkness in my reflection

I look into the glass,
no longer recognizing
The depthless eyes looking back at me,
that hold in them the burden of being
Dark swelling circles underneath
like permanent horizons
without a sun

His enigmatic gaze peers back into me
In him I feel defeat, absolute
hopelessness
and I watch
as he puts a gun to his own head
I can't understand
why.

My hushed screams, unreachable
desperately I plead
for someone to stop him, but I know
I am the one
that must save him
the only one who can

Hospital

Nausea. Bright lights. Sharp pain
Emergency hallway   careful steps forward
Dazed delirium
Passing from one person to another
"What seems to be the problem sir?"
Date of birth. Address. Insurance. Copay.
"Sign here sir"
"Please wait over here sir"
Waiting hall heavy with strained silence
My name is called, sickened eyes turn towards me

Pass through double doors. Clean. Too clean
The air tastes metallic. Cold sweat trickles
down my back. Shivering
they tag me. I lay on a bed of stone.
Doctor walks in, tall and gaunt.
"What seems to be the problem?"

Heartbeat. Blood pressure. Temperature. Check
Hooked up to machines. Metal monstrosities
reflect pale overhead lights
"Your finger here please. Your arm please. Look here"
"Say ahh please. Turn your head this way please"
"Does this hurt?"
"Scale of 1-10 please. Thank you."

The abrasive tune of machines, beeping.
Results are in
"Looks like you have…"
Nurse comes in. Bitter taste of medicine lingers.
I lay back on the stone bed, stare at patterned ceiling tiles
The halls filled with dormant murmurs and idle chatter
The pain slowly subsides,

The world stops shaking, the tremors fade.
Time to escape this factory, that turns the miserable
slightly less harrowed

I've grown wings

Father Time, toyed
with the flow
of past   years
to make them feel unending
robbing the fickle sanity from my warped mind

All the wounds I've incurred
the self-inflicted,
the betrayal, the loss
wounds this world has branded me with,
I wear them all like precious mementos
of a past i'd rather forget

the anguish
led my metamorphosis
I've shed the enfeebled spirit that once cocooned
this body
I've grown ebony wings that can handle
the shrill winds of tomorrow

I witnessed the world ignite
escaped the fires that would engulf me
and from below I watch

with Love, Death and Time

Flightless

Unwritten story

We're all insignificant
specks, in the universe's immortal novel.
In a book of infinite perpetuity
we fill the blank space, everyday, a sentence or a word,
Its pages filled with an infinite swarm of finite lives,
an unfathomable myriad of melding of tales
Innumerable fates colliding in entropy

beginning and ending in a blink

Has anyone ever opened this novel
and gazed into the boundless eternity
Peered into the core of our existence, beyond human
Dimension. Has god read this novel, flipped through
the interminable pages with poised fingers
Does he chuckle at the futility of human life
at the tragic irony of human actuality

Tonight, I celebrate another day
on this strange voyage
Another day survived.
Tonight, the moon whispers a lullaby,
it's time
to delve into a slumber so sweet
it emulates death
and helps me forget

A note in the melody of darkness
It took me two years to tell you
that his death
killed
me
too.
I'm plummeting
like the tumbling mirth of a lark
flying too close to the ground
I'm a teardrop of morning dew
slowly tracing blades of grass, slipping into soil,
absorbed for roots to take life from.
I'm being drained by this world.
My right eye sees no sunlight.
I'd like to understand the nature of falling
and I know I avert my eyes instinctually
when I tell you I've landed softly in the night
curled up in its somber song
and became a note in its seductive melody

The train tracks call out to me
The starry canopy that spoke to me
through twilight whispers
only reminds me

of the unbearable weight of existence
There is no sky in my dreams
but slumber cannot erase
the bitterness of being from my tongue.

A knife is not a weapon
it's a savior.
Do you know why
my wrists bleed in my daydreams?
It's because train tracks call out to me
and I long to feel
2000 volts make my heartbeat surge
so I can feel alive
in my final moments
of perishment

Sovereign of the abyss

In this Hell, from which I've manifested
years ago, or millennia now,
In this Hell, that echoes the sweet aria
of tortured souls,
that weaves a cacophonous melody
of harpy claws grating against tender flesh,
In this Hell, where hope
is a dangled jewel for the naive
and a temptation for the brave
In this Hell, where the sirens of suffering
multiply and form symphonies of torment
In this Hell, where love
is a myth, conjured by Lucifer's eternal tauntings
to play minds into an endless spiral of lonesome yearning,
In this Hell, where not even light escapes,
In this Hell,
consumed by loathsome, ebony flame,
I reign, as sovereign of the abyss
For I have witnessed and felt
all of its harrowing insanity,
and I have survived

Paradise built in hell

It's not that I've fallen
for the darkness swimming through
the red rivers in my thin slitted veins
but these days I feel
the pain

is a different kind of pleasure,
a suffering indistinguishable from ecstasy.
Days and nights pass without
sun or moon
I feel safe
listening to a silent song rewind despairing

thoughts, as if Satan's black nail is
twirling around the scratched record that contains
the next soul he seeks to devour.

Sunlight hurts, splits my mind
like clouds after rain storms, corrupted
by black hearts on fire still wanting it all.
I'm not enamored by the agony

But some nights when I sit alone,
face to face with my shadow,
I cannot tell whether he's begun to smile

Notes & Reflections

I dedicate the epigraph of this book to my father, who was a brilliant writer, but never got the chance to publish his works before passing away. With this, I honour the memory of a great poet the world lost the opportunity to truly discover. The poems in the chapter, "High flight abandoned", are all dedicated to both my father and Dr. Bill Anderson who was both a mentor and family to my mother and I.

I believe it is in a poet's nature, in similar fashion to a magician's, not to reveal what's behind the curtain, to hide the meticulous effort through which they intricately craft every tiny detail of their poems, through which their true beauty blossoms. It is mercy for the audience not to reveal what's behind the magic, so as not to disillusion them or to restrict the limits of their creative imaginations. I believe a tiny peek behind the curtain, to see the magician preparing, always breeds greater appreciation.

The footnote under "The world robbed me of you" was inspired by something my professor, Shara McCallum, once said: "In poetry, the further away the mask is to you, the closer it is to you." I mulled over her words in the back of my mind for months until the concept was born—that my poetic persona (for whom I've adopted the pen name "Le Prince Héritier" or simply refer to as "The Poet," both names I've inherited from my late father) is shaped by both my "true" face, my inner mind that attempts to hide its misery, and my "mask" that I wear to conceal my true face, which has now blossomed a life of its own. In my poems, I switch between using "I" and "i", which denote the two different aspects of my persona. The word "I" is used approximately 346 times throughout this book, eventually I can

151

no longer tell who in me is speaking through the voice of these poems.

This book is a collaboration between the younger versions of me as a poet, since pre-adolescence, who contributed all the raw emotion for this book, and the current me, who offered the technical skill to refine the voice of every piece.

"Black Boy, Ebony Wings" was a poem I had originally written in French, when I was fifteen, while studying abroad and facing segregation and racism on a scale completely foreign to me. The original poem is lost on scrap paper somewhere, but I later recreated this liberation poem in the wake of American controversy.

In "African pride," I allude to many different aspects of my family's culture, such as: naming ceremonies, the West African deity Ifa (Orunmila), regarded as the deity of wisdom, palm oil (which I love), shea butter (which I wear on every sunny day), and Yoruba, my mother's language.

"Black Wallflowers Don't Blend" is a title inspired by the movie title *The Perks of Being a Wallflower*, which is one of my favorite coming of age movies. In this piece, I pay homage to the languages of my infancy that have left me in my assimilation to western culture. I also pay respect to those who protest discrimination and police brutality by kneeling before the national anthem.

"Poem for parkland" contains a nod to the seventeen moments of silence, observed by the House of Representatives, as well as the moments of silence and mourning observed by protesters and family across the country.

152

"Lost in our interstellar" was inspired by a close friend of mine, who studies astronomy. My favorite line in the poem is "radiating midnight rays, only visible/to the dark-adapted." I feel this line encapsulates the two of us and our connection more than any other line, and it captures fully the beauty of science, which I am passionate about as well. The imagery in this poem was all inspired by a recent phenomenon in the scientific world: the first observable merger of two neutron stars ever detected (event GW 170817). It is theorized, without any conclusion reached at this time, to have either produced the most massive neutron star ever recorded, or a black hole with the lowest mass.

"The girl I met in April" is a poem inspired by the Japanese animated series "Shigatsu Wa kimi no uso" which translates to "Your lie in April" written by Naoshi Arakawa, with heartbreaking music by Masaru Yokoyama.

"Lovers destiny" pays homage to Eshu, a Yoruba/Fon deity, the divine messenger. The line "the white thread that lead us…" was inspired in part by a work of art by artist Mio Hanaoka, entitled "Melancholy (The White Thread of Fate)." The line "resow our fate with red thread" is in reference to the Japanese legend of the red string of fate (赤い糸).

"The story in her eyes" was written about my most guilty of pleasures: silence.

"Fated Flight" is modeled after John Magee's "High Flight," the first poem I ever fell in love with.

"Nowhere Origins" is a poem to answer the question "where are you from?" which I never have the patience to answer in full. The poem connects every place in the world I have deep ties to,

153

even if forgotten in my infancy, the imprint is still somewhere in me.

"Anxiety is a noose" has a nod to my favorite children's writer, Shel Silverstein, author of *The Giving Tree* and many other classics such as *Where The Sidewalk Ends*. He often hides tragedy and very morose themes in his children's literature. This piece has no punctuation, as anxiety and mental illness take no breaks in me.

"Imagine" is the first poem I ever had published. It was written during a period of controversy over transgender rights to use public bathrooms that match with their gender identity. It was re-edited shortly after President Trump's transgender military ban. The poem was passed to someone who identified as transgender for review before being submitted for publishing—an important step for many of my poems that deal with issues that do not directly affect me personally. There is also a reference to Project Semicolon, which is an organization dedicated to suicide prevention, an issue very close to my heart.

"Our Rising Voices" was written in two parts. The first was written on Donald Trump's inauguration day (January 20th 2017) and the second, during the monumental Women's March, which I had the immense fortune of participating in two days later. The latter half was also modeled after Maya Angelou's renowned poem, "Still I rise."

I wrote "At your wake" on a plane after my grandmother's wake, in tears. She spoke to me at her wake, I heard her voice, and this is one of three poems I wrote in response.

"Beautiful stranger do not fall" begins with a quote from my current favorite novel, *The Angel's Game* by Carlos Ruiz Zafón. This quote, in part, inspired the concept of this poem.

"Savior complex" is a poem I wrote when I was around fifteen, and at eighteen, I reworked it as somewhat of a satire piece critiquing my own masculinity and savior complex.

"Ode to the romanticization of Death" was inspired by one of my favorite novels, by José Saramago entitled *Death with Interruptions*, which offers one of the most intriguing and romantic depictions of death that I have yet to ever read.

"Hospital" was written while I was in a hospital bed, doubled over from a stomach virus. I asked the nurse for a pen and paper, settled for sticky notes, and wrote through the pain.

"A note in the melody of darkness" is also inspired by John Magee's "High Flight," but this poem is its antithesis and serves as a contrast to my earlier poem "Fated Flight."

"The train tracks call out to me" was written, in contemplation, in front of train tracks.

"The cup we drink from" was inspired by some of the most eye opening words by Khalil Gibran that resonated with me.

Every Khalil Gibran quote was taken from Andrew Dib Shefran's novel *Khalil Gibran: The Nature of Love* and Khalil Gibran's *The Prophet*, published by Alfred A. Knopf.

"All I have to do is remember her smile" has one specific line inspired by works by Rumi. The line is: "She loved him/Beyond existence."

"Chasing sunrises" was modeled after the song "Syre" by Jaden Smith, which is also the name of his musical, anti-hero alter ego.

"I was named 'devotion' in a past life" was inspired by Rudy Francisco's poem "Chameleon." It invited me to be more introspective about my own motivations, breaking away from the tunneled naïveté of my younger self's outlook for a moment, and allowing my poetry to challenge the different dimensions of my emotions of longing and desire.

One of my favorite things to insert into my poems are lines that remind me of what song(s) I was listening to while writing. Music is a great trigger for memory, so I italicize these lines so that when I reread them I can hear the music in my mind and it takes me back to the moment.

The line: *run from the blue lights* was inspired by Jorja Smith in her song "Blue lights," in which she commands *Don't you run when you hear the sirens coming.* The visuals from her song have since inspired many of my poems on black resistance.

The line: *Tempted to pursue the precious memory of you still* was inspired by Hozier's song "Better love," which is easily one of the most lyrically beautiful pieces of music I can name.

The line: *I am the dry desert rose he'll try and press/between two pages* was inspired by the chorus to Lolo Zouaï's 'Desert rose': "Love me like a desert rose." She is a bilingual singer of Franco-Algerian roots. Desert roses are rose-like crystals that forms in the deserts of Algeria.

The line: *Her lips would be my favorite getaway/A sweet disaster* were inspired by John Legend and the group DREAMERS. I find both of these 21st century musicians quite poetic in their

156

own respective ways I like the contrast between Legend's poised eloquence and the authentic, unapologetic, youthful recklessness of DREAMERS.

"We are only flawed" was inspired by Morgan Parker's amazing poetry collection *There are more beautiful things than Beyoncé* which struck me through my core so intensely that I wrote a set of poems in the margins of my copy and managed to get one of them into my book the day before my deadline. The way in which she examines and expresses her womanhood really touched me and allowed me to feel more comfortable as a man who continually seeks to challenge his own concept of what it means to be a man, and whose body, at times, questions whether it might feel more naturally at ease as a woman.

Not a single poem in this collection ends in a period, my story is not yet done, but I've just embarked on this strange voyage.

Every dimension of this poetry book, from the cover to the autobiographical photo on the last page and the page arrangements, represents the duality of the two souls that exist in me now. I've begun to cherish them both preciously.

Acknowledgments

Grateful acknowledgment is made to the publication that published my first poem and has since published half a dozen more — Weasel Press: Voices for Peace: "Imagine"

I must first thank my father, who named me and helped raise me even in the time after his passing. My poetry would not exist without him and my ambitions began with a promise to achieve what he did not have the opportunity to before he left. I want to thank my family who never stop being supportive and amazing.

My deepest gratitude to Shara McCallum, my poetry professor, who taught me more about poetry, its beauty and infinite possibilities, than anyone else. The success of my edits are attributed to her guidance and teachings. I'd like to thank all the teachers who supported my beginnings in poetry and the friends who always showed excitement towards my poetry and always filled me with positive energy.

Special thanks to my friends from my poetry class and my friends from Penn State's W.O.R.D.S club, who reinvigorated my love for writing and helped strengthen my confidence in my poetry. I am incredibly indebted to my amazing editors, who've been super patient with me and the fluctuations of my poetic growth, without their dedication this book could not have happened.

About the Author

Photo credit: Elena Cadenas

Sankara "Le Prince Heritier" Olama-Yai currently lives near DC. He is of African descent, born of Beninese and Cameroonian parents. His passions include traveling, art, songwriting, film and occasional Netflix bingeing. He has two forthcoming poetry books with Vital Narrative Press to be published in the following calendar years. His writings and poetry attempt to explore globally controversial issues, while giving an introspective look into the author's mind and a critical view of society and human nature. His poems have been published by Rising Phoenix Press, Weasel Press, Literary Yard, InSpiritry "Building Bridges-Making Peace", Military Experience and the Arts "Blue Streak", and other publications In addition to having won four Scholastic Art & Writing awards for poetry and short story writing.

161